Rhapsodies

Two Plays

by Rosary Hartel O'Neill

A Samuel French Acting Edition

New York Hollywood London Toronto
SAMUELFRENCH.COM

Copyright © 2009 by Rosary Hartel O'Neill

ALL RIGHTS RESERVED

CAUTION: Professionals and amateurs are hereby warned that *RHAPSODIES* is subject to a Licensing Fee. It is fully protected under the copyright laws of the United States of America, the British Commonwealth, including Canada, and all other countries of the Copyright Union. All rights, including professional, amateur, motion picture, recitation, lecturing, public reading, radio broadcasting, television and the rights of translation into foreign languages are strictly reserved. In its present form the play is dedicated to the reading public only.

The amateur live stage performance rights to *RHAPSODIES* are controlled exclusively by Samuel French, Inc., and licensing arrangements and performance licenses must be secured well in advance of presentation. PLEASE NOTE that amateur Licensing Fees are set upon application in accordance with your producing circumstances. When applying for a licensing quotation and a performance license please give us the number of performances intended, dates of production, your seating capacity and admission fee. Licensing Fees are payable one week before the opening performance of the play to Samuel French, Inc., at 45 W. 25th Street, New York, NY 10010.

Licensing Fee of the required amount must be paid whether the play is presented for charity or gain and whether or not admission is charged.

Stock licensing fees quoted upon application to Samuel French, Inc.

For all other rights than those stipulated above, apply to: The Marton Agency, 1 Union Square, Suite 815, New York, NY 10003; Info@MartonAgency.com.

Particular emphasis is laid on the question of amateur or professional readings, permission and terms for which must be secured in writing from Samuel French, Inc.

Copying from this book in whole or in part is strictly forbidden by law, and the right of performance is not transferable.

Whenever the play is produced the following notice must appear on all programs, printing and advertising for the play: "Produced by special arrangement with Samuel French, Inc."

Due authorship credit must be given on all programs, printing and advertising for the play.

ISBN 978-0-573-69769-2

No one shall commit or authorize any act or omission by which the copyright of, or the right to copyright, this play may be impaired.

No one shall make any changes in this play for the purpose of production.

Publication of this play does not imply availability for performance. Both amateurs and professionals considering a production are strongly advised in their own interests to apply to Samuel French, Inc., for written permission before starting rehearsals, advertising, or booking a theatre.

No part of this book may be reproduced, stored in a retrieval system, or transmitted in any form, by any means, now known or yet to be invented, including mechanical, electronic, photocopying, recording, videotaping, or otherwise, without the prior written permission of the publisher.

MUSIC USE NOTE

Licensees are solely responsible for obtaining formal written permission from copyright owners to use copyrighted music in the performance of this play and are strongly cautioned to do so. If no such permission is obtained by the licensee, then the licensee must use only original music that the licensee owns and controls. Licensees are solely responsible and liable for all music clearances and shall indemnify the copyright owners of the play and their licensing agent, Samuel French, Inc., against any costs, expenses, losses and liabilities arising from the use of music by licensees.

IMPORTANT BILLING AND CREDIT REQUIREMENTS

All producers of *WINGS OF MADNESS* and *TURTLE SOUP* must give credit to the Author of the Plays in all programs distributed in connection with performances of the Plays, and in all instances in which the titles of the Plays appear for the purposes of advertising, publicizing or otherwise exploiting the Plays and/or a production. The name of the Author *must* appear on a separate line on which no other name appears, immediately following the title and *must* appear in size of type not less than fifty percent of the size of the title type.

CONTENTS

Wings of Madness......................................5

Turtle Soup..........…............................13

WINGS OF MADNESS

WINGS OF MADNESS premiered at The Producer's Club in New York City, May 2006

CHARACTERS

CLAUDIA, a beautiful woman of uncertain age, pale-faced with long blonde hair. Her voluptuous figure is sheathed in moonbeam silk.

SETTING

The interior of a Spanish-type mortuary on Veterans Highway outside New Orleans, the type with fake brick, too much wrought iron, and lanterns with amber glass or possibly glass in several colors. Tackiness is felt in the details: an overdone sign-in table, metal folding chairs, a pressed wood end table with Kleenex and plastic roses, and a coffin.

The coffin may be placed in the audience.

(A forbidding July night. It is raining; claps of thunder rumble the cheap building. Outside, the highway is full of sinister noises, gusts of wind, the slush of water, car brakes, muffled screams. The interior of the room is in complete darkness except for the vigil lights on the sign-in table. Candles flicker in their ruby glass cups. **CLAUDIA** *appears, framed in the doorway. A wispy chiffon scarf floats free in the breeze which blows from behind her.* **CLAUDIA** *points to her gown.)*

CLAUDIA. What's this? The latest in shrouds. *(Turns around, shows her half-covered back and bare feet)* No back. No shoes. I don't worry how I dress because people don't look at you long inside a casket in New Orleans. This is the city that care forgot!

(LIGHTS: CLAUDIA *flicks on a light.)*

CLAUDIA. There's a young man laid out in parlor B, who won't say a thing. Those moody people from the Ninth Ward. I've to accept I've more education than he has. We're not going to speak. He'll never be from uptown. Why couldn't I have been buried from Bultman's—the mortuary on the avenue that's like a plantation? They know how to showcase a body. *(Somberly)* When I think of it pouring on my tombstone... my little patch of dirt.

(SOUND: *A truck approaches, then passes.)*

CLAUDIA. Trucks racing outside. A Taco Bell next door. I don't know anyone who uses a mortuary on Veterans Highway. *(Inspecting the parlor)* Tigerlily Kleenex boxes on every table, a blanket of plastic roses. *(Points to her casket)* And cheap lining, flamingo pink. *(Gingerly picks up the sign-in book)* Well, who do we have here? Death brings all the relatives out. *(Sadly)* Even in the rainy days of July.

(SOUND: *Noises, hushed talking, and approaching footsteps.)*

CLAUDIA. My family's at the door. They're sure enough late.

(SOUND: *Muffled noises, talking, a harsh male laugh.)*

CLAUDIA. My husband, Elliot. He smiled once or twice, and he was nice once or twice. If he gets any fatter, he'll lose his looks. They call him the walrus 'cause he flops about. Elliot was homeless once, for seven or eight months, but it's okay now, he drives a Mercedes. He's got that jaundiced eye, from listening to the funeral director tally up the expenses. It was an extensive make-over. The man's got money, but he's not used to giving it to a mortician. *(To Elliot)* Come here, my hubby. Up close, you can see my eyelid wrinkle. My hair's still growing. Death's so messy. *(To Marguerite)* There's my little girl, Marguerite. Behind her daddy. That haircut looks awful, Marguerite. Never show those ears. *(Sadly)* Remember when I plaited your hair in ten thousand itty-itty braids, and I left it like that for the whole summer. Stay back. Better not see me up close. You've got my pictures. All those Christmases and Easters when I looked so pretty. Elliot, take her away.

*(**SOUND**: The startled soft cry of a child, which intensifies as **CLAUDIA** speaks.)*

CLAUDIA. Stop the sniveling, Marguerite. We need gentlemen and ladies, even at the mortuary. Pretend graciousness. You'll always be missing something, Marguerite. A mother who's weak is no role model for a daughter. I'm just a little stone in the river that you pass to move on. Look, I want you to stand over there by the wall. Think pleasant thoughts. I'm experienced in dealing with grief. That's my strongest point. Life's going to sling disappointments at you. So if you start out sad, you're already in trouble. Stay back. We mothers have got to go one by one. Perfectly normal procedure. God can't kill everybody at once. It's too expensive.

*(**SOUND**: Whirl of cars passing. Heavy rain. A little girl shrieks.)*

*(**CLAUDIA** raises her hand as if admitting a secret to quiet the child.)*

CLAUDIA. Your father said I fell off the roof of that six floor building. But I didn't. *(Pause)* I was pushed. However, fair's fair. I provoked him first. Never touch a man in anger, sugar. They always hit back. Hard. It's not their fault, really. It's a testosterone thing. Can't have the little woman shoving them around. Carelessness has become so rampant. *(Pause)* I dove like a winged chariot. No back-up. No props. Someone carted my remains over here. The soul is left to linger after a violent death. Spirits don't come and carry you aloft.

*(**SOUND**: Bolt of lightning. Crash of thunder.)*

(Marguerite howls.)

*(**LIGHTS**: Lights rattle off and on.)*

CLAUDIA. Stop crying, Marguerite! I don't want to live again. Marriage is a curse. It both lifts you up, and gives men a vantage to shoot you down. Once you make marriage everything, you have the smell of desperation.

*(**SOUND**: Mozart's "Requiem" is played.)*

*(**CLAUDIA** laughs hoarsely, running her fingers wildly through her hair, enjoying the music and moonlight.)*

CLAUDIA. How lovely. I've such energy under the moon. Daddy told me he was faithful, again and again until I believed him. Before I go to Hell, I've one chance to avenge him. To have someone's name is to have some control over his soul. So, I'll roam around. Then, on an ugly night when Dad's got his hands on some pretty young thing, I'll appear like a phantom wife, clutch his throat with my cold, withered hands and choke out his life. *(With a nervous chuckle)* Rain's stopped. Time to slip inside my mahogany box. Close the lid. Waiting's a tedious job, but I'll be back.

CURTAIN

TURTLE SOUP

CHARACTERS

UNCLE GENE SONIAT, age 69

LUCILLE, his niece, 29

SETTING

The present time, April 1st, in New Orleans.

(Noon, the present time, April 1st, in New Orleans. A stark light glares into the master bedroom of a mansion. A clever man, **UNCLE GENE SONIAT***, 69, lies on his sickbed. Deaf, he stares blankly ahead, and breathes through a partially opened mouth. When he speaks, he shouts. His pregnant niece,* **LUCILLE***, 29, enters with a tray of soup and calls out nervously over his rough breathing.)*

LUCILLE. Uncle? Uncle? I'm coming in? I brought you turtle soup from the Country Club. It's marvelous to think someplace still makes great soup. Turtle soup was a specialty of the late-nineteenth-century café society. It contains a strained broth and turtle flesh. Are you breathing? Don't die while I'm here! *(Calls out)* Nurse! Nurse! Where did the nurse go? *(Puts the soup on a table with legal documents; picks up one; talks to herself)* What's this? A new will?

UNCLE GENE. It's hot!

LUCILLE. Oh, Uncle! You scared me! *(Slips the paper back)* No fever. But you're sweating. I'll fold back these sheets. It's ninety degrees outside. The humidity creeps in.

UNCLE GENE. Have you seen the helicopter?

LUCILLE. You've been dreaming, Uncle. Eat something.

UNCLE GENE. Helicopter's landing.

LUCILLE. Some turtle soup.

UNCLE GENE. What?

LUCILLE. *(Hollers)* From the Country Club!

UNCLE GENE. You didn't charge that to me?

LUCILLE. They don't...take cash. This delicate soup with flesh will restore your strength. No other soup is finished with sherry.

UNCLE GENE. Huh?

LUCILLE. If you dined in Victorian society, you'd likely start with turtle soup. It's event eating like going to a three-star restaurant in Paris. I got the Club recipe from Cook. Take the flesh of one shelled, skinned, and cleaned turtle. About two pounds of flesh. In a soup kettle, cover with four—*(***UNCLE GENE** *spits it out)* Oh. Don't spill it. Good Lord. Nurse!

UNCLE GENE. *(Shouts)* Did you put my car up?

LUCILLE. I didn't drive it.

UNCLE GENE. Where're my keys?

LUCILLE. Where I left them yesterday.

UNCLE GENE. Who's got my keys?

LUCILLE. They're the most famous keys lost in New Orleans. Twenty people looked before finding them. I bet they're where I left them—

UNCLE GENE. What's that?

LUCILLE. We'll try some later. *(Swallows hard, wipes her brow)* Uncle…Uncle Gene, I need you to…improve…so you can help with the baby.

UNCLE GENE. Huh?

LUCILLE. The pregnancy's fine. I've the doctor's advice in this book. *(Holds up a book)* We're naming the baby after you. But I don't know where to put the nursery. I thought we might use that sewing room for—

UNCLE GENE. What's that?

LUCILLE. (*Screams*) The baby!

UNCLE GENE. I don't want a baby. Don't bring it here. Southerners worry me. We're dealing with a smaller and smaller gene pool. Hah! So much soup, and none for me. *(Pointing)*

LUCILLE. Sure. You don't want more fresh soup? By the twentieth century, most turtle soup is canned. It stopped being a big American soup 'cause the soup's popularity endangered turtles. But a private organization like the Country Club could—

UNCLE GENE. Huh?

LUCILLE. *(Shouts)* Make turtle soup!

UNCLE GENE. Since I knew your dead mother and father, I take the liberty of telling you, you've soup on your teeth. Hah!

LUCILLE. Well? I'll...just wipe my...mouth...Uncle? My husband...asked me to speak to you. I need your help...with finances. Can I talk to you...Would you explain these...You've never told me about your investments, securities?

(She takes out some papers. **UNCLE GENE** *hits his hand against the bed. He makes an awful grunting sound.)*

UNCLE GENE. Arf. Arf. I can't hear a word you're saying!

LUCILLE. Money's due on these—insurance policies.

UNCLE GENE. What's that?

LUCILLE. *(Shouts)* Premiums. Am I authorized...to pay them?...I don't have power of attorney.

UNCLE GENE. Debutantes. You don't go to the bank. The money's supposed to appear in your purse.

LUCILLE. I'm trying to...to manage the household and medical expenses. Upkeep is costly. The chairs need reupholstering. The doorknobs should be replated, and the ceiling medallions—The entire house needs painting...

UNCLE GENE. I just gave...the Dominicans...ten stained-glass windows...in honor of...my mother and father...and the deceased...Soniat-Nix family...members. Arf! Arf!

LUCILLE. Are you choking? Nurse! Shouldn't someone be here? Where's Father Boileau? Doctor Jayne? Uncle...I hate to bother you with my troubles, but I lost that teaching post. I pray to God the delivery's easy because I've no medical insurance. We have my husband's unemployment, thank God, though it's running out. He auditions—but in a freelance business, the question is, "Who wants to work with you?" An actor—

UNCLE GENE. Huh?

LUCILLE. *(Shouts)* An actor!

UNCLE GENE. All that effort for temporary work. Hah! What's he done? A couple of movies people are afraid to see...They place his films in the rear of the store! That ought to tell you something...You'll be lucky if you don't get a disease. What will it take to bail you out?

LUCILLE. Your attorney says you've...added a codicil...to your will.

UNCLE GENE. I can't hear what you're saying.

LUCILLE. Oh, your hearing aid is in the wrong ear. It's the left ear, not the right. Why did you do that? *(fixes the hearing aid)* Can you hear me now? You hear?

UNCLE GENE. Don't shout.

LUCILLE. Your lawyer is concerned...

UNCLE GENE. My lawyer.

LUCILLE. She says you've...left all your money to the Dominicans.

UNCLE GENE. You came here to weasel your way—

LUCILLE. Did you give my inheritance—

UNCLE GENE. To bother me...with your selfishness?

LUCILLE. I want to know if you've cut me out...before I see you...in your casket!

UNCLE GENE. I can leave my money to whomever I want.

LUCILLE. It's not that I want the...the money. It just makes me feel...If I didn't know better, I'd think I was a stranger...and that my life had been a dream. I would care for you...even if you lost everything. But you do nothing for me.

UNCLE GENE. Don't get worked up!

LUCILLE. I think of you as my father and since I've moved up here, I've admired you.

UNCLE GENE. I took you off the street. Isn't that enough?

LUCILLE. Yes, but living here you made me feel I was your daughter.

UNCLE GENE. I never adopted you.

LUCILLE. I'm your only living relative.

UNCLE GENE. I raised you and gave you a house.

LUCILLE. Which is falling apart. My father was your only brother!

UNCLE GENE. Come on. My estate's not worth much…after taxes…hospital charges…about…

LUCILLE. Nine million.

UNCLE GENE. I'm a millionaire. What do you know?

LUCILLE. Don't mock me.

UNCLE GENE. Has your no-count husband been tracking my assets?

LUCILLE. He talked to an estate specialist.

UNCLE GENE. Did he? Why don't you give me the name, so I can find out how wealthy I am.

LUCILLE. We promised not to…but it's the most reputable firm.

UNCLE GENE. What's its name? Hah!

LUCILLE. They estimated the value of this house, your country home, your French Quarter apartment, your commercial properties: Pizza Hut, the phone company, the post office, that Canal Street parking lot—conservatively at ten million.

UNCLE GENE. How did they inflate their figures? Here's how I see it. Your actor husband walks into this big house on Exposition Boulevard and finds a sick old man and a plain young girl. This actor's well has run dry, and his future is behind him. *(Clutches his chest)* Bad indigestion. So the actor takes a look at the ugly girl and considers marriage. "What's wrong with her?" he thinks. She ought to be fun. Did she stop ovulating? Change zip codes? At first, the thought of marriage hits hard. He doesn't want a "bouder" wife. A pretty, pouting wife, but he thinks he does. He's not broke, you see. He's having a hard time meeting the standards he's developed. And he likes that house. He thinks, "Why not marry this girl and take the old man's money? The fellow can't last that long."

LUCILLE. Liar!

UNCLE GENE. I'm cutting you out of my will. I don't owe you a damn thing. And I hate this darn soup! *(Dumps the bowl of soup upside down)* Get out, and get my nurse. I would hate to meet my maker after treating me so unfairly.

LUCILLE. May you burn in hell.

UNCLE GENE. *(Points to heaven)* I'm going up. The Dominicans are getting me in. And when I go there I'll be right next to St. Peter. There are no places in heaven. Now I may have to fry longer in purgatory. But when I arrive, I'll have Christ on my left and Saint Peter on my right. *(Clutches his chest)* My chest! I can't breathe. Call Doctor Jayne… Father Boileau. I need to say my Act of Contrition. Get a priest…you idiot! *(Coughs and laughs uncontrollably)* I didn't change the will. April Fool!

CURTAIN

ABOUT THE AUTHOR

ROSARY HARTEL O'NEILL is the author of fourteen plays produced internationally by invitation of the American embassy in Paris, Bonn, Tibilisi, Georgia, Budapest, Hungary, London and Moscow. Her play UNCLE VICTOR was chosen Best New American Drama by the Cort Theater, Hollywood, and celebrated in the Chekhov Now Festival in New York. BLACKJACK was selected for Alice's Fourth Floor Best New Play Series. She was founding artistic director at Southern Rep Theater from 1987 to 2002. She has been playwright-inresidence at the Sorbonne University, Paris; Tulane University, New Orleans; Defiance College, Ohio, the University of Bonn, Germany and Visiting Scholar at Cornell.

Other fellowships include the Virginia Center for the Creative Arts (VCCA) Playwrighting Fellowship to Wiepersdorf, Germany, and two fellowships to the Playwriting Center, Sewanee University. She also received a play invitation to the Actors Centre, London, as well as residences in playwriting at the VCCA, Ragsdale, Dorset Arts Colony, Byrdcliff Arts Colony, and the Mary Anderson Center.

She was chosen outstanding artist in Paris and awarded a Fulbright to Paris for her play WISHING ACES. She was a finalist in the Faulkner Competition for New American Writers; a finalist for outstanding artist for the state of Louisiana 2002; and a finalist in the Ireland Tyrone Guthrie Residency in playwriting with the VCCA 2002. She was awarded a Senior Fulbright research specialist in drama to Europe, 2001-2006, and received first invitations to the Conservatoire Nationale du Drame (leading acting-training center in Paris) and the Conservatoire Nationale de la Danse (leading dance training center outside Paris).

Recent professional achievements include: DEGAS IN NEW ORLEANS, which was invited to the New End Theatre (a heralded theater for contemporary plays) in London and featured in the Best New American Play Oktoberfest of the Ensemble Studio Theatre (a leading theater for new work) in New York City and in the Reading Series of the Abingdon Theatre, New York. She is playwright-in-residence at the National Arts Club, where much of her recent work has been developed

SAMUELFRENCH.COM

THE OFFICE PLAYS
Two full length plays by Adam Bock

THE RECEPTIONIST
Comedy / 2m, 2f / Interior

At the start of a typical day in the Northeast Office, Beverly deals effortlessly with ringing phones and her colleague's romantic troubles. But the appearance of a charming rep from the Central Office disrupts the friendly routine. And as the true nature of the company's business becomes apparent, The Receptionist raises disquieting, provocative questions about the consequences of complicity with evil.

"...Mr. Bock's poisoned Post-it note of a play."
– *New York Times*

"Bock's intense initial focus on the routine goes to the heart of *The Receptionist's* pointed, painfully timely allegory... elliptical, provocative play..."
– *Time Out New York*

THE THUGS
Comedy / 2m, 6f / Interior

The Obie Award winning dark comedy about work, thunder and the mysterious things that are happening on the 9th floor of a big law firm. When a group of temps try to discover the secrets that lurk in the hidden crevices of their workplace, they realize they would rather believe in gossip and rumors than face dangerous realities.

"Bock starts you off giggling, but leaves you with a chill."
– *Time Out New York*

"... a delightfully paranoid little nightmare that is both more chillingly realistic and pointedly absurd than anything John Grisham ever dreamed up."
– *New York Times*

SAMUELFRENCH.COM

BLUE YONDER
Kate Aspengren

Dramatic Comedy / Monolgues and scenes
12f (can be performed with as few as 4 with doubling) / Unit Set

A familiar adage states, "Men may work from sun to sun, but women's work is never done." In Blue Yonder, the audience meets twelve mesmerizing and eccentric women including a flight instructor, a firefighter, a stuntwoman, a woman who donates body parts, an employment counselor, a professional softball player, a surgical nurse professional baseball player, and a daredevil who plays with dynamite among others. Through the monologues, each woman examines her life's work and explores the career that she has found. Or that has found her.

www.ingramcontent.com/pod-product-compliance
Lightning Source LLC
Chambersburg PA
CBHW070651300426
44111CB00013B/2366